Do You Believe?

IN THE MIRACLE WORKING POWER OF GOD

Jiangy C. Moore

ISBN 979-8-88685-584-5 (paperback)
ISBN 979-8-88685-586-9 (digital)

Christian Faith Publishing
832 Park Avenue
Meadville, PA 16335
www.christianfaithpublishing.com

Printed in the United States of America

Acknowledgments

Writing a book is not an easy task and can be very daunting. I am grateful to the Almighty God for His grace and inspiration through His Holy Spirit. I especially want to thank my children, Kendrick, Gianna, Gabrielle, Kiersten, Kristi and Hannah—my *cheerleaders* and support team. Special thanks to my parents, John and Memay. My beautiful mother for telling me the story of my birth and upbringing, thank you. Thank you to all my siblings especially Johnetta, Ledyitee, Beletiah and Luwai. My friends, coworkers, Brandywine Home Therapies and church family at RCCG Amazing Grace who contributed to this work, thank you. Lastly, thanks to everyone on my editing and publishing team.

Introduction

Are you at a place where you feel like the whole world has forsaken you? Maybe you are saying to yourself, *This is it. This is the last resort. This is my stopping point. If I don't get the answers I need from reading this book, I'm done following or believing in God.* I am here to tell you that you were not led to this book by mistake but rather guided by the Lord. The purpose of this book is to bring life back to a situation that is dead, hope to the hopeless, encourage the brokenhearted, and bring healing to the wounded in hearts. In this book, I am sharing my testimonies of the goodness of God in my life as a child of God and what faith and patience in God can do. The Bible tells us in Psalm 145:4–7,

> One generation shall commend your works to another, and shall declare your mighty acts. On the glorious splendor of your majesty, and on your wondrous works, I will meditate. They shall speak of the might of your awesome deeds, and I will declare your greatness. They shall pour forth the fame of your abundant goodness and shall sing aloud of your righteousness.

My prayer is that my testimonies will affect and be an encouragement for my generation and the generations to come and to let someone know that no matter what you're going through in life, no matter how big the battle is or how hard the wind and the storms of life are hitting you, if you believe in the Almighty God, He can turn your situation around for His glory. I pray that the Holy Spirit will guide my writing and lead me into your hearts, in Jesus's mighty name, amen.

There's a song by Tim Godfrey ft. Travis Greene, a Nigerian musician, called "Nara" that says: "What the Lord has done for me I cannot tell it all," which is the case for me. Looking back at my life, starting from my birth (as narrated by my mother), the Lord has been very gracious and good to me. This is not because I'm righteous or because of any works that I have done or will ever do but because He is God. However, I will try to share all that the Holy Spirit reminds me of.

The fact that I am writing this book, I am blessed. The fact that I have the gift of life—I can breathe freely, and I can walk, talk, and sing—I am blessed. I can no longer continue to allow shyness to hold me back day by day, week by week, month by month, and year after year from testifying to the goodness of God in my life. That would be very ungrateful of me because, truly, God has been and is so good to me. In 2 Timothy 1:8 it says, "Therefore do not be ashamed of the testimony about our Lord, nor of me his prisoner, but share in suffering for the gospel by the power of God." It's not because of who I am or what I've done but because of who He is.

Chapter 1

The Story of My Birth

Writing to you is a little girl who came from a humble beginning. My mother is from a two-mud house village in Liberia, West Africa, called Po Town. My father is one of thirty-two siblings from a polygamist family in Liberia, West Africa. Through the divine favor of God, my father was fortunate to land a good job at the airport in Liberia and travel frequently to America. I was born in September 1978 as the second daughter to the union of my parents, John and Memay. My sister, Johnetta (Mercy), and I are one year apart. When my mother found out she was pregnant with me, my father had just been granted a two-year scholarship in America at the Chanute Air Force base in Rantoul, Illinois, to study weather forecasting. This was a special training sponsored by the United Nations at that time. Whenever he was on break from school, he would travel back to Liberia for visit and then return to the United States.

According to my mother, her pregnancy for me was somewhat of a surprise as she did not know she was pregnant. She said that she was getting sick frequently and losing weight. She went to the doctor but was told she was not pregnant. As it is the norm in most African countries, when modern medicine cannot figure out the cause of an illness, people will usually consult native doctors or herbalists. So on the advice of a trusted family member, my mother said she was taken to see an herbalist who told her that she was bewitched. He said that whoever bewitched her was spiritually draining her blood, and that is why she was getting ill and losing weight.

My mother said the herbalist told her that she will die as soon as her blood drained from her body. She said she was still attending school. So one day, while at school, in the midst of all the other students during devotion, she suddenly felt dizzy, dropped on the floor, and became unconscious. She said when she gained consciousness, she found herself in the principal's office. She was informed that her schoolmates picked her up from the floor and brought her to the office. The principal sent her to see a doctor in the city, who informed her that she was pregnant. So this is how she found out she was pregnant with me and started receiving prenatal care.

She said when she went into labor for me, my father was already back in the United States to continue his training. She was home alone, and the only person around who was available to help her was my father's elder brother, Sam. He called a cab to take her to the hospital and sat with her in the back of the cab. While en route to the closest hospital, driving on a dusty unpaved road, she went into full labor and delivery, delivering me in the back of the taxis cab, right in his hands.

My mother was very young and inexperienced and did not know what to do with the baby. She received no prenatal care or education. They continued to the hospital hoping for further care and treatment. When they arrived at the hospital, she was put in a room on a very hard table with the midwife and nurses attending to her screaming at her to push out the after birth. She was clueless as to what they were talking about so they left her there. After a while, she was able to deliver the afterbirth or placenta while she was alone in the room. The staff came back and transferred her to the postnatal unit.

The next day, the other postpartum women in the unit were given meals, but they did not give my mother any meal. She asked for food and was told they have to check their roster to see if her name was on the list before she could be served. After checking, she was informed that her name was not listed, so they could not give her food. She was left in that room for three days, not given any food or water to drink. After the third day, she requested for her baby so she could leave as she did not see the need to remain in the hospital. The hospital was located in a very sandy area. She put me on her shoulder and started walking to the cab station to wait on a cab.

Think about this for a moment. She had just given birth with no food or water for three days, yet she was walking in a sandy area. She said she remembered walking and falling down with me, getting up, walking, and falling again out of exhaustion, hunger, and thirst. Looking back and picturing the scenario, a lot of things could have gone bad. She could have been so exhausted, passed out from dehydration or heat, and collapsed over me—her three-day-old baby. I could have died lying under her helpless body from suffocation or sudden infant death syndrome, or even stolen from her arms.

Wow, talk of sacrifice! What a sacrifice my mother made for me to be here in this world. My prayer is that the LORD will grace her with strength, good health, and long life to receive the celebration she deserves and to enjoy the fruit of her womb. I am truly honored to be one of her daughters.

Mommy, you are the best mother in the whole wide world!

The Lord tells us in Isaiah 41:10, "So do not fear, for I am with you; do not be dismayed, for I am your God. I will strengthen you and help you; I will uphold you with my righteous right hand." Indeed, the Lord was with my mother and me on that faithful day, renewing her strength and upholding both of us in His righteous right hand. May God bless her heart and the hearts of every mother reading this book.

So back to the story, she managed to reach the cab station. She sat on a log by someone's shop, waving for a taxi cab at a very busy intersection, but none stopped. She waved and waited, waving and waiting, to no avail. As she waited, she said she noticed from the corner of her eyes, far off in a distance, a caterpillar truck with a driver and one passenger in the front seat. She said, as they got closer to her, she heard the passenger say to the driver, "Stop, stop, stop. That's my baby's mom!" The driver stopped the truck immediately, and the passenger got out of the car, ran to her, and asked her where she was going. She said she was going to town where she would get another taxicab to take us home to Robertsfield. He assisted her with getting a taxicab to take us home. When she got in the car, the song that was playing on the radio station was "Sweet Mother" by Prince Nico Mbarga. He was a highlife musician, born to a Nigerian mother and a Cameroonian father in Abakaliki, Nigeria. To summarize, the lyrics for this song are,

> Sweet mother I will never forget you for the suffer you suffer for me. When I cry my mother carries me and say my child, stop crying, when I want to sleep my mother comforts me, lays me down well, covers me with a blanket and says sleep my child. When I am hungry, my mother runs up and down to find me something to eat, When I am sick, my mother cries and begs God to help safe her child from dying. When I don't sleep, my mother don't sleep; when I don't eat, my mother don't eat; she does not get tired. Sweet mother I will never forget you for the suffer you suffer for me. You can get another wife, another husband, but not another mother.

What a message in this song. God speaks to us in so many different ways. As I was writing, it now dawned on me after all those years that this was a message and instruction God was giving to me to remember the suffering my mother endured at my birth. I pray the LORD for His mercy over my life.

They did not ask her for any of her personal information, name, or where she lived. But to her surprise, the next day, the two men came looking for her and brought with them everything a newborn would need, from diapers and food to clothing, and departed without giving any information about who they were. From that day till now, she never saw them again and never knew their names or who they were. She's tried searching over the years but has never found them.

In the neighborhood, an elderly woman who visited my parents frequently came by to visit and to welcome the new baby. When she heard the story surrounding my birth, and the scholarship my father received around the same time, she came to the conclusion that I am a blessing and a lucky child to the family. She suggested that my name should be Jiangy (pronounced *Jan-jay*). My father is of the Bassa tribe, and my name is a Bassa name. In English, it means *blessings* or *a gift from God*.

This is the story of my birth and how I was named. She said another neighbor also gave me the name Joan, which is of Hebrew origin, which also means *God is gracious*. As the meaning of my name goes, so has my life been—truly a blessing. The Almighty God has been extremely gracious and loving to me. Tell me now if those men were not angels of the Almighty God. Scripture tells us that God commands His angels to charge over our lives according to Psalm 91:11–12,

> For He will command His angels concerning you to guard you in all your ways. On their hands they will bear you up, lest you strike your foot against a stone.

Some evil occurrences used to happen when I was a baby. She said she made my bed on the floor, which was the norm back then, and would hear a female voice in the middle of the night calling me to go with her. She said she would experience heaviness, preventing her from getting up. But I was protected by the divine protection of the Almighty God.

Chapter 2

God Speaks in Dreams and Visions

In 1982, my father was traveling to the United States, and my mother was accompanying him on that trip. I was only four years old, and my sister was five years old, and we could not travel with them at the time. So my sister and I were left to be raised by my mother's elder brother and his wife. They had six children of their own and were raising other family members' children as well. There were a total of eighteen people in a four-bedroom house that we all helped build. My parents decided to settle in the United States of America to explore other opportunities.

By age seven and eight, my parents brought my sister and me to join them in the United States, but that was short-lived. Two and a half years later, in 1988, they got a divorce. My mother started a new relationship and soon moved out, leaving my sister and me in the care of my father. After she felt she was settled in with her new life, she requested my sister and me from my father. I remembered her working two jobs and taking my sister and me to one of her friends' house where we would stay all day after school, through half of the night, and she would pick us up around midnight.

She was still fairly young, with two young children, and thought the best decision at that time was to take my sister and me back to Liberia to stay with her brother. So my mother took my sister and me back to Liberia unbeknownst to my father and left us there with the same uncle who lived in Kakata, thinking it was for our best interest at the time.

My mother eventually got remarried and had three children, my other siblings, whom I love dearly, Ledyitee, Beletiah, and Luwai. I am one of six children from my mother's side and one of seven from my father's side.

When we got to Liberia, we were introduced to my stepfather's relatives living in the capital city, Monrovia. Whenever my sister and I were on break from school, we were sent on vacation to Monrovia. While in Liberia, at the tender age of ten, I started experiencing some unusual things that I could not understand as a child. God began showing me things through dreams that would come to pass exactly as I dreamed it. The Bible makes us understand that God can speak to us through our dreams.

> At night when people are asleep, God speaks
> in dreams and visions. (Job 33:15 GNB)

> This is what I will do in the last days, God
> says: I will pour out my Spirit on everyone. Your
> sons and daughters will proclaim my message;
> your young men will see visions, and your old
> men will have dreams. (Acts 2:17 GNB)

Every time I was in Monrovia, God would show me all the witches and the witchcraft activities in that family we were vacationing with through visions and dreams. An innocent little girl as I was, with no spiritual inclination, I would wake up and tell the same people what was revealed to me in the dreams God showed me. For this reason, every time I went there, I would get really sick. I experienced severe itching over my entire body as if something was crawling under my skin. As I scratched, long marks would appear on my body. I was frequently rushed to the hospital in the middle of the night for treatment. Without conducting any testing, the doctors were calling this strange illness filaria. I called it a strange illness because immediately when I left the city and returned to Kakata, I would recover from it.

I remembered this one dream to today's date very clearly. The relative we vacationed with was married with four boys and a four-month-old daughter. He and his family shared one bedroom along with his sister in their father's house. They had one full-sized bed in the room. His sons and sister slept on the floor on a mat while he, his wife, and infant daughter slept on the bed. When my sister and I visited, my step-uncle slept in the living room, and my sister and I slept on the bed with his wife and daughter. My sister would sleep on the front edge of the bed, followed by me next to my sister, then the infant daughter, and the mom next to the daughter. We were all crammed together like sardines in a can, touching each other with no way to change position as we slept.

One night, we all went to bed, and everyone fell asleep but me. I could not fall asleep from the room being extremely hot. As I was lying down, I saw the door to the room flung open as if a force came against it. I felt a presence and heaviness over my entire body that paralyzed me instantly. I saw a black ghost-like cloth floating through the door, coming over me, and stopping when it got on top of the infant daughter. I tried screaming and moving my body but to no avail.

While it was floating over the baby, I saw the baby's soul lift from the bed to the black cloth, and it floated with her out the door, and the door flung shut behind them. That's when I could move. I screamed and woke everyone up and told them what happened. A couple of days later, after my sister and I left, we heard the baby got seriously sick and died. I was about eleven years old when that happened and still remember it to this day.

> The LORD shall preserve thee from all evil:
> he shall preserve thy soul. (Psalm 121:7 KJV)

Indeed, the Lord kept me during those times and continues to keep me from all harm.

Chapter 3

Living in a Civil War

One year after being back in Liberia, at the tender age of eleven, in December 1989, a civil war broke out in the country that lasted approximately fifteen years and claimed millions of lives. I lived and survived four years of that war, living in fear for my life, being raped or taken by rebels as a sex slave. I slept in bushes with layers of clothes on to be ready to flee at any time. I remember walking for days and getting to rebels' checkpoints where they were using human skulls for light, jumping over bodies, and seeing the elderly being left behind because they were too weak to make the journey.

There were days when we had no food to eat. I could no longer endure such conditions as life had become too unbearable for me at that young age. I remember this one day, asking my sister to kill me. I told her that I did not want to commit suicide because it was a sin against God, and asked if she can please take a stick and kill me. I was tired of the constant fear of being raped, forced into child marriage by the rebels, and getting killed running. Thankfully, my sister responded by saying, "God said we should not commit murder, so I don't want to sin against God as well." You, know, the Word of God says in Psalm 121:7,

> The Lord will keep you from all harm—He will watch over your life.

By His special grace and protection, I was not harmed. He preserved me because He had a special plan and purpose for my life, like He does for each of His children.

In 1993, by this time I was fourteen years old, and the family I was living with fled to a neighboring country for refuge, namely Ivory Coast, Côte d'Ivorie.

We had been on the road for a couple of days trying to get to the border shared by Liberia and the Ivory Coast from Nimba County. The Cavalla River, also known as the Cavally the Youbou or the Diougou, separated Liberia and Côte d'Ivoire. As God could have it, we arrived safely but were not permitted to cross because it was late, and the bridge was closed for the day. We were about eighteen in number traveling. They gave us a small room to sleep in for the night.

While sleeping in the middle of the night, the border was ambushed by one of the rebel groups. We were awakened by the sound of various kinds of gunshots and people screaming and running to get over the bridge. The Ivorian guards were encouraging us to run over for safety. We ran as fast as our feet could carry us, leaving everything behind. Again, by the special grace of God, we were able to cross the bridge safely and arrived in Ivory Coast. We went back for our belongings when the situation got under control.

Chapter 4

Life as a Refugee

On arrival in the Ivory Coast, we were escorted to the refugee camp established at their border for Liberians fleeing the war where we registered to receive food, medical aid, and other essential supplies. The camp was in the town of Danane. We registered for school after being out of school for about two years. However, because the country is a French-speaking country, we were told that we would have to study French for one year before enrolling in school. Because our schooling had already been delayed as a result of the civil war, my mother did not want any further delay. So she instructed that we go to Ghana instead, which is an English-speaking country.

Not knowing anyone in Ghana, or what to expect, we left as instructed, which was a struggle in itself. On arrival to Ghana, we were dropped off at the front of the refugee camp in Buduburam. We were taken to the registration center at the Women's Center. The center was closed because we arrived late in the evening. It was an open center, with no doors or windows that could be closed. It was a place used to train women in trade skills, like sewing and tie-dyeing. Students attending the refugee school also used the facility as a study hall and recreational center.

As I said earlier, we had no relatives and did not know anyone at the camp. So we were preparing to spend the night at the center until morning to register. Upon registration, families were given food and supplies ration and a plot of land and were provided with some necessary materials like cement and black roof tarpaulin to build their own house to shelter their families. The night had fallen, and we were each finding our position on the training tables in the center to rest for the night. We had not eaten for the entire time we were traveling, which was about two days. We had no water, food, cooking pots, pans, or utensils. But the Almighty God, our Heavenly Father, said in Deuteronomy 31:6,

He will never leave us nor forsake us.

So while getting ready to sleep, we saw a lady walking by. Immediately, she saw us. She ran over and greeted us as if we were related, or she had known us for a very long time. She introduced herself as Margaret and insisted we follow her home. She had a one-bedroom house. We were eighteen in number, so her home could not accommodate all of us, including herself. She made arrangements with some of her friends for additional lodging and gave us food to eat. May the Lord remember her for her kindness and selflessness toward us.

The King James Version tells us in Psalm 46:1,

God is our refuge and strength, a very present help in trouble.

He uses each of us in different ways to be that help for one another. So it is important to heed His call for your brethren. The morning came, and we were able to register with the United Nations High Commissioner for Refugees (UNHCR). We were given the necessary allocations, along with a plot of land. We built, with our own hands, a four-bedroom house. Margaret allowed us to stay in her home until our home was completed. Everyone who was of school age registered at the refugee school on the camp. I was fifteen years old and in the tenth grade at the time. I was so excited to be starting school again.

Education has always been very important to me. It was the first day of school, and all the students gathered for morning assembly in line formation, per grade, in front of the individual classroom door. I have always been a very shy and timid person, so I stood quietly in line. Then I heard a quiet voice in my ear saying, "Would you like to be my girlfriend? You don't have to answer me right now, but please think about it." I was shocked, happy, and scared at the same time because it caught me by surprise. I was so afraid of boys at the time because my uncle was very straight in our upbringing. We grew up in the church and were not allowed to talk to boys. So I turned around to have a glimpse of who the voice was coming from and saw a very tall, probably about six feet, skinny, handsome young man with beautiful pink lips standing behind me. I am five feet and one inch tall, so I had to look up to see him. I told him I would think about it and let him know. I felt good knowing that a boy found me attractive. I thought about it and agreed to be his girlfriend.

So he was officially my first relationship. We were both fifteen years old, so young and innocent but enjoyed each other's company and loved each other very much. After a year of attending the refugee school, my mother enrolled my sister and me in a boarding school in Accra, Ghana, called Nungua Secondary School. So I rarely saw *my first love*. He was sent to a different boarding school as well by his parents. During breaks, we would go back to the camp. However, he often left for Ivory Coast, where he stayed until school resumed. We wrote letters to each other and spent time together when we had the opportunity.

All this time, my father did not know the whereabouts of me and my sister since the outbreak of the civil war whether we were dead or alive. My mother was still struggling and healing from the divorce, not knowing what my father's reaction would be knowing we were caught up in the war. She thought it would be best if my sister and I never try to communicate with our father. In order to get her point across, she said if we do, then she would stop all support for our upkeep.

However, my sister and I did not listen to her on that point. Every time anyone we knew was traveling to America from the refugee camp on the resettlement program, we would send letters through them to our father. In the letters, we told him where we were and that our mother does not want him to know anything about us. We sent letters for over a year with no response, but we never gave up in hopes that one day one of those letters would reach him.

I prayed silently that God would answer our prayers and that one of those letters would get to my father. My sister is a pessimist and always focused on the negative aspects of things, which can be very discouraging at times. So I kept my hopes and prayers to myself. Job 33:14–15 says,

> For God does speak—now one way, now another—though no one perceives it. In a dream, in a vision of the night, when deep sleep falls on people as they slumber in their beds.

One night, God showed me a dream. In the dream, we were on campus, and it was a typical weekend. Students were standing on the balcony, some had visitors and were sitting under the trees next to the front gate of the campus, some were doing laundry and ironing their clothes for the week, and others were walking back and forth from the dormitory to the classrooms to study. My sister and I were walking across the field in the middle of campus, heading back to the girls' dormitory next to the front gate. As we approached the front, I saw the gateman open the gate, and a taxicab drove in and stopped right in front of the dormitory. I saw a man get out of the car from the front passenger side, and I immediately recognized it was my uncle we were staying with. I ran as fast as I could to the cab and saw my dad sitting in the back seat. With excitement, I opened the door and shoved myself in, landing on his lap and screaming, "Daddy! Daddy!" Then I woke up from the dream.

It felt so real! I told my sister the dream, and her response was, "That will never happen. That was just a dream, so don't put your mind on it." I guess, in a way, she was only trying to protect me as her younger sister so I won't be devastated if it was only *just a dream*.

Having faith in the miracle-working power of God is extremely important. Faith is what moves God to action because His name is on the line. So I continued to pray on it and trusted the Lord that one day, in His time, He'll bring that dream to pass. A couple of days went by after the dream, and one day, our uncle paid us a visit on campus to tell us he had a surprise for us. He said he cannot tell us what the surprise was until we see it. Deep in my heart, I just had this feeling that it had to be the dream that my dad was going to surprise us by coming on campus, but I kept it to myself.

If you are reading this book and maybe going through one circumstance or another that is proving to be impossible, if you are at the point of giving up and letting go of God, I just want to encourage you to trust in the Lord and continue to hold onto Him. It is in the impossibilities in our brokenness that God is testing our faith in Him and want to show Himself strong in our lives and those around us.

The Bible says in 2 Chronicles 16:9 (KJV),

> For the eyes of the LORD run to and for throughout the whole earth, to shew himself strong in the behalf of them whose heart is perfect toward him.

God being God, the dream was fulfilled exactly as it was shown to me. In 1995, we were reunited with our father after seven years of having no contact.

When my father arrived at the school in Accra, Ghana, he met with the school's principal or headmistress, as she was called Ms. Bannerman. He introduced himself to her and asked her to kindly look after my sister and me. He said, moving forward, he would be responsible for our upkeep and the tuition. He asked her permission to take us off campus to spend some time with us. She was kind enough to allow us to leave campus to spend time with our father.

Those few days were the best time I had had in the last seven years. The vacation was soon over, and my father had to return to the United States. From that moment on, Ms. Bannerman took care of me and my sister as her own daughters. My father did the best he could to support us. Unfortunately, due to life circumstances in the States, my father was unable to attend to our financial needs all the time on a timely basis. So from eleventh to twelfth grade, it was a struggle to pay the tuition and school supplies.

At the beginning of the school year, when students were returning, the principals and office staff would sit at the front entrance to receive the tuition before you were permitted to stay. They would look up your name and announce loudly the amount you owed, and if you didn't come with the amount, you would be sent away with all your belongings. Talk of embarrassment.

The Lord assures us in His Word according to the New Living Translation in Proverbs 3:4,

> Then you will find favor with both God
> and people, and you will earn a good reputation.

The Lord is a good God and an excellent Father who takes care of His children. His Words concerning you are *yes* and *amen*. "For all the promises of God in him are yea, and in him Amen, unto the glory of God by us" (2 Corinthians 1:20).

I remember standing in the line, with my heart pounding, as if it will pop out of my chest if care is not taken. Standing there, my sister and I did not even have a single food item for the semester or a dime for school fees. We would get to the front of the line and be called forth individually. They would check the list, double- and triple-check the list, but neither my sister nor my name would be found on the list. Wow! Talk of the divine favor and grace of the Almighty God that caused Ms. Bannerman's heart to find favor in us.

Though she had two wonderful children of her own, Louise and Patrick, she assumed the relationship of my sister and me as though we were her own. May God bless her heart and may that same favor rest upon her and her children's life. I attended the entire three years tuition-free. In addition, she would give us allowances, food, lodging when school was not in section, and transportation. To God be the glory.

Chapter 5

All Relationships Are Not Ordained by God

Four years after living as refugees, my sister and I were joined with our father in the United States of America. I was almost nineteen years old and had just completed high school. Coming to the United States came with its own challenges. My father was not in the best living condition. He was struggling financially with no reliable means of transportation. But someway, somehow, he got us to where we needed to be. He made sure we always had our needs met. He taught us how to adapt to our new life in America and gave us the keys to be successful in this great land.

He would always say, "My daughters, take education seriously. Men will come and go in your life, but what you learn, no one can take away from you. It may not guarantee you the job you want but will give you options." One of his favorite lines was, "No condition is permanent."

As we went through the struggles, those were his words of encouragement. These are valuable pieces of advice that I live by today and pass on to my children. I remember my father would come home from work and sit with me and my sister at the table, going over different educational opportunities he saw in the newspaper to see if it were something we were interested in learning. We would dis-

"

cuss the pros and cons of each of them. The next day, he would make phone calls to set up appointments with the various institutions.

After deciding on which career pathway I wanted to follow, I registered and was accepted into a cooperative nursing program. At a very young age, I wanted to be a medical doctor. So making the decision to attend nursing school first came fairly easily, and I was eager to get started. After starting school, my father would advise us to always check the bulletin boards at school for any scholarship opportunity to help finance our education. Though he was experiencing financial hardship, he insisted that my sister and I should focus on our education instead of working, and he did what he could to keep us afloat.

My older sister connected with her childhood friend, who came to visit and brought a friend along. They spent the weekend with us and went back to their place of residence out of state. After they left, the friend reached out to me via phone, and it birthed a long-distance relationship. We dated on and off until I met my son's father. Seeing that the long-distance relationship was not getting anywhere, and there was no true commitment on his part, I decided to call it quits and settled with my son's father. So needless to say, at age nineteen, I started my first long-term relationship.

After two years since my arrival in the United States, I started taking college courses. However, I became pregnant at age twenty-one and gave birth to my first child (Kendrick). Through the special grace of God, there was no interruption in my education. I pursued and completed the registered nursing program through pregnancy.

The relationship between my son's father and me started out great, but over time, it became toxic. My son's father was very hardworking, working double shifts during the week. On weekends, when he was not working, he would spend the time drinking and partying with his friends. But whenever he got drunk, "all hell broke loose" as they say.

Being from the African culture, we are taught to handle family issues through our parents and or our pastor; getting the cops involved is something that is frowned upon. Needless to say, my parents and his mother were called upon very frequently. I knew I had to get out of the relationship, but I did not have the willpower to get up and leave.

Long story short, I remembered praying to God, saying, "Father, if this relationship is not of You, please remove my son and me from it." I prayed that prayer every day for a while, believing that one day, God would answer my prayer and deliver me. To the glory of God, I remember one evening we had a minor dispute in comparison to others we've had, and he grabbed a large black garbage bag, opened the drawers and closets, and put all my clothes and shoes in it. He loaded his car with it.

All the while, I sat on the bed thanking God, praying in my heart that as he's packing my things, God will cause him to pack my son's things as well. My son was a year and a half at that time. Then I saw him grab another bag and put all my son's clothes in it as well. He put the things in his car, grabbed my son and me, and put us both in the car, saying, "I'm taking you back to your father's house." He drove us there, put our things in my father's house, allowed us to get out of the car, and he sped away.

I said, "Thank You, Lord, for answering my prayers." The next day, he realized what a big mistake he had made, but it was too late, and that is how God separated me after four years. Occasionally, I would take my son to visit to spend time with his father since he was fairly young. On one of those visits, I saw my son's birth certificate on his end table that I had been searching for, thinking I had misplaced it in the process of moving. So when he was not looking, I took the envelope with the certificate, put it in my bag, and went home with my son. After that day, I took my son again to visit with his father and on another day after I got home from work. We did not have a custody order in place at that time. He tried begging me to come back to him, but I was not giving in to his request.

When he realized he was failing in convincing me, he got really upset and demanded that I gave him back the envelope with my son's birth certificate. I pretended I didn't know what he was talking about. He got extremely angry. I put my coat on and my son's so we could start leaving. I had my wallet in my coat pocket. He reached out to take my wallet out of my pocket, demanding that he will cease it until I returned the paper, which I needed to register our son for school. I had my driver's license and other important things in my wallet. Knowing that when he gets a hold of it, I would probably not get it back, I put my hand in my pocket and held tightly onto it. He grabbed my pocket from the outside of my coat and dragged me all around the apartment to take my wallet while our one-and-a-half-year-old son watched, crying.

While I was being dragged, he accidentally injured his hand and released my pocket. This was the moment of escape God had given me. I quickly got off the floor, grabbed my son, and ran downstairs. When I looked back, he was pursuing me. With no time to put my son in the back of the car in his car seat, I put him in the front passenger seat. By this time, he was right behind me. I left the door ajar and ran around to the driver's side. I had my right hand resting on my son to keep him from falling. I started driving with my left hand as his father was hanging on the front passenger door. I drove slowly until he couldn't hold onto the door any longer and let go. I drove to where it was safe and properly secured my son in his car seat. Talk about panic attack and posttraumatic stress syndrome.

I was hyperventilating all the way home. Every time I saw a car behind me that looked like the one he drove, my heart would start to beat rapidly. I got home and could not even get out of the car because I was shaking so bad and afraid he had followed me, which he did.

He was making verbal threats and so forth. I remained in my car and called the police in fear for my safety and that of my son. When he realized I had called the police, he left before they arrived. I got out of the car after he left, went inside the house, and realized he had injured my shoulder in the process. My shoulder hurt so bad that I could not remove it an inch from my body. That was the last time I visited him and got a custody order in place.

Unfortunately, he passed on when our son was thirteen years old. May his soul rest in peace. By the grace of God, prior to his passing, God created the opportunity for me to tell him that I have forgiven him and asked for his forgiveness as well and that I am very grateful. I have to give credit to his mother who was always very supportive of our relationship. She treated me as her daughter, even up until now, and always volunteered her services whenever I needed help even after her son and I separated. She was the first face my son saw when he was delivered and hers were the first hands that held him. So he grew a special bond with his grandmother.

She offered to take my son and raise him so I could continue my education. But because I was not raised by my parents in the earlier part of my life, I did not want my son to experience that as well. So I turned down her offer. But even with that, she would come to the house every day and help me with caring for her grandson, cooking, cleaning, and anything else I needed. She just wanted me to focus on my schooling. May the LORD remember her for her sacrifice and continue to comfort her heart on the loss of her son.

Forgivingness is something that we all struggle with but one that is very important in the eyes of God and for our salvation. No matter the pain, hurt, or trauma, God commands us to forgive one another. This is by no means to downplay anyone's hurt or pain. Forgiveness is good for your soul and acts as a key to your deliverance and allows God to begin to act on your behalf. It is the key to unlocking the door to the next phase of your life. So let go and let God take it over. Trust me, I can relate. It is not easy and does not happen overnight, but it requires daily steps. Lean on the grace and strength of the Almighty God to carry you through. All He desires for you is the decision and commitment to forgive. One way or another, we have all done something wrong through the course of our lives and desire forgiveness, whether from God, ourselves, our spouse, family members, or friends.

Matthew 18:21–22 says,

> Then Peter came to Jesus and asked, "Lord, how many times shall I forgive my brother or sister who sins against me? Up to seven times?" Jesus answered, "I tell you, not seven times, but seventy-seven times."

Tomorrow is not promised to any one—believers or nonbelievers. Forgiveness is impossible after death, and you do not want to live with the guilt of, "If I had known." God, in His infinite mercy, granted me the opportunity to forgive my son's father before his passing, but it may not be the same for you. If you are reading this, the LORD is asking you to forgive. I pray that He grants you the strength, willpower, and courage you need to forgive whoever may have hurt you in your journey of life that you, too, may be forgiven, in Jesus's name.

Time went by, and I reconnected with my long-distance friend. I told him I was looking for a committed relationship, and if that wasn't the case for him, then it was best we remained separated. He said he was ready to commit, and so the relationship was rebirthed. He later enlisted in the Marine Corps of America and was deployed to Iraq and Afghanistan on several occasions. After several years of dating off and on and not seeing the relationship progressing, I went to God in prayer. I asked the LORD if this relationship was His Will for me, and if there was anything that I needed to know, He may reveal it to me.

It is written in Jeremiah 33:3 (KJV),

> Call unto me, and I will answer thee, and
> show thee great and mighty things, which thou
> knowest not.

If there is anything concerning your life that you are not sure of, remember this scripture. Go to the LORD in prayer and watch Him unfold the mystery to you.

Needless to say, in 2006, God answered and uncovered what was being kept in secret, and that was the end of that relationship. Broken is an understatement! I was broken to the point where I was on the verge of depression, but God rescued me yet again.

Seeing how broken I was, my cousins would invite me to outings to take my mind off things. Every year in July, Liberians in the United States gathered together for a three-day weekend celebration, in observance of Liberia's Independence Day every July 26. The celebration includes a ballroom dance on Friday, a soccer game on Saturday, followed by an after-party, and a cookout on Sunday. So on Saturday, July 22, 2006, Liberians within the tristate area—New Jersey, Pennsylvania, and Delaware—gathered in West Windsor, New Jersey, for the soccer game.

After the game, I went home with no intention of going anywhere else. I changed my clothes, took a shower, and went to bed. Around midnight, I received a call from my cousin and friends insisting that I accompany them to the after-party. I told them I was not feeling up to it, and as a matter of fact, I was already in bed. They kept insisting no matter how I refused. Still trying to convince me, they said, "Just come over and hang out with us so you're not alone."

Reluctantly, I agreed. I threw on some regular clothes and drove to my cousin's house. To my surprise, when I arrived at her place, they were all dressed to go out. Again, I said I was not feeling up to it, and neither was I dressed to go anywhere. But the Bible makes us understand that the devil is very crafty in all his dealings. Despite my persistent refusal, they still offered a solution.

So one of the girls living at my cousin's house went into her closet and found me an outfit. I quickly changed, and we left. It is important to ask God for wisdom to see and understand the devices of the devil. We got to the after-party in town, but the people in the crowd were much younger, and it was *boring*. We got back in the car. By this time, it was one o'clock in the morning. For me, this was good news. I could drop them off and go home. But that would not go down that easy.

They started calling other friends around in search of another party. They were informed of a bridal party in someone's basement. They insisted that we go, and because it was my car and I am not a drinker, I was the designated driver. I drove everyone an hour from Trenton, New Jersey, to Philadelphia. It was at that party that I met the man I would later marry.

Going back a year before we met, I attended a revival. We were instructed to come with a special seed and our prayer request on the last day of the revival. I took my *seed* and my prayer request as instructed. A prayer point was raised to talk to God about your request. So I proceeded to pray and tell God that I want to be married by the next year, 2007. I gave God a full physical description of who I wanted with no mention of any spiritual attributes. You may think I am crazy, but getting married was very important to me because I had planned my life ever since I was about eight years old.

At that young age, I planned that I was going to finish high school; go to college; and upon graduation, would get a job in my field of study; and then get married and start my family. I achieved all my education and career goals, so I felt it was time for me to get married. Looking back, there were several important lessons I learned from this whole scenario. The first lesson is that God will sometimes put obstacles before us to make us turn around from going the wrong direction or to protect us from deviating from His path, which is what happened leading up to the party.

The second lesson is that sometimes putting a demand on God to do what we want Him to do, at the time we want it done, can be detrimental to our life, soul, and destiny. God is our Father. Before He chose who our parents would be and created us in our mother's womb, He had a plan for each of our lives. This, He said in His Word in Jeremiah 29:11 (NIV),

> "For I know the plans I have for you,"
> declares the LORD, "plans to prosper you and
> not to harm you, plans to give you hope and a
> future."

At no point in my prayer request did I ask God what His plan was for me, concerning marriage or even for a sign. Remember the story in Genesis 24 when Abraham sent his servant to his relatives in Mesopotamia to find a wife for his son Isaac? In Genesis 24:14 (GNB), the servant said to the LORD, "I will say to one of them, 'Please, lower your jar and let me have a drink.' If she says, 'Drink, and I will also bring water for your camels,' may she be the one that you have chosen for your servant Isaac. If this happens, I will know that you have kept your promise to my master." The Bible says it was late in the afternoon when he got there, the time when all the young women came out to get water. This leads me to believe that many beautiful women came through. But Abraham's servant asked God for a specific sign and waited patiently for the sign, which was confirmed when Rebecca arrived at the well.

The third lesson I learned is that whenever you have a burning desire for something you are praying and trusting the Lord for, the devil will try to rush ahead of God by bringing an answer that checks all your boxes. It is in those moments that it is important not to be carried away by excitement but rather go back to the Lord and ask for wisdom on how to proceed.

Lastly, I learned that God's timing is not our timing, and waiting on God patiently is very important. Patience is a virtue lacking in many believers. The lack of patience has caused and is causing many people to make poor choices, thus opening the wrong door. Having patience can be difficult, but the Lord is our strength when we are weak. We only just need to ask Him.

So everything I asked God concerning my future husband at that revival, I saw in the man at the party. We dated briefly, and he proposed within six months of meeting. With my lack of patience and the desire to get married and start my family, I accepted without asking God for wisdom on how to proceed, or confirmation if this man was sent by Him. But before and after the engagement, there were so many questionable things and red flags that I ignored. God tried to warn me through so many different people, but I wanted what I wanted and did not listen to God speaking.

Needless to say, nine months after the engagement, we got married and immediately started having children. The marriage quickly became very toxic, again. I was physically, verbally, mentally, and emotionally abused, controlled, and isolated from family and loved ones. I was manipulated throughout the course of the marriage. I remembered being pushed through a wall, leaving a hole in it and injuring my arm. There was a time I was shoved in a tub of water at three months pregnant and left there gasping for air. On many occasions, I would have to run between my children's bedrooms and hide under their beds or closets in fear for my safety, just to name a few. There were also a lot of infidelities.

After seven years of marriage, my husband suggested that we relocate from New Jersey to Frisco, Texas. He said there were a lot of distractions where we were, the cost of living was high, and the move will give us a fresh start. So as a person who always valued marriage and family, I was willing to do whatever it takes to save my marriage and keep my children in a family unit. Needless to say, I agreed to the relocation.

We packed up an entire house, transferred the children out of school, left a great-paying management position, and moved across the country. By then, we had two high schoolers, a first grader, and a preschooler. The only support we had was his sister and her family. To not be a burden, I took an overnight staff nurse position with one of the local hospitals. Things went well for the first few months. It seemed like the marriage was getting back on track, but that was short-lived.

A person will always be who they are unless they sincerely repent of their ways and cry to God for transformation. If their mindset remains the same, changing location will not make any difference. Two months after the move, I discovered I was pregnant. Conditions became drastically worse. I was under tremendous stress to the extent I was visiting the emergency room every week, looking so disheveled. Diagnosed with gestational diabetes and stress, I was being treated for having a high-risk pregnancy. My husband moved out of the house to his sister's place, taking his teenage daughter so I would be left with no assistance.

In my condition, I was left to care for three minor children. I was broken in every way. I felt trapped with no way to get out. I cried myself to sleep most nights with the LORD being my only consolation. I kept praying, asking God to change him and for God's intervention. But the reality is, no one can change another person.

Jeremiah 13:23 (GNB) says,

> Can a Nubian change the colour of his skin,
> or a leopard remove its spots? If they could, then
> you that do nothing but evil could learn to do
> what is right.

So only God has the power to change a person. For this change to happen, the person must truly confess his/her wrong behaviors, acknowledge they exist, and sincerely apologize for them to God and the people he/she has hurt.

Chapter 6

Trusting in God's Plan

A lot of times, we don't want to do this; instead, many of us want to blame our wrongdoings on someone else. This was the case with my marriage. So I cried to the LORD. I asked Him for mercy. I pleaded with Him for help and direction. I knew I had to leave; otherwise, my unborn child and I would be dead, and my children would be left without a mother. I thought the best option was to move back to New Jersey for myself and my unborn child's safety, as well as my other children until I give birth.

Moreover, I had my family there to lean on for support and lot of professional networks for employment. But then I thought, *What employer will hire a three-month-high-risk pregnant woman, requiring weekly doctor's visits and or hospital admissions and at the same time the primary caretaker of three minor children?* The devil is really good at reminding people of their limitations and barriers as a distraction from God's path. He does this by using the spirit of fear.

But 2 Timothy 1:7 (KJV) lets us know that "God has not given us a spirit of fear, but of power and of love and of a sound mind." So I said, "LORD, You are the God of impossibilities. If this is Your will, please direct me."

I remember getting to work at four-thirty in the morning and just praying in my heart for direction. My breakfast break came at eight-thirty. I sat in the break room, and the LORD spoke to my spirit to call my former manager in New Jersey from a previous company of employment. I was hesitant at first, but the pressure would not go away. So I obeyed, picked up my phone, and called. By the grace of God, she answered.

With my heart pounding, I said, "Hi, this is Jiangy, calling to see if you have any open position. I moved to Texas six months ago, but things are not working. My marriage is crumbling. I am three months pregnant, high risk, in and out of the hospital twice a week, and raising three minor children, and I need to move back. I need a job to provide for my children and medical coverage, and the LORD put you on my heart to call you. Can you hire me?"

There was a silence on the other end of the line, and all the doubts came rushing back in my mind. Then the silence broke. She said, "Jiangy, you would not believe this, but I have been asking corporate for months now for approval to hire another nurse, and they have been denying my request." She went on to say that she just opened her email and saw that her request had been approved. She was sitting and thinking where she is going to find an experienced nurse who is reliable for the position. Suddenly, her phone rang, and it was me looking for employment. She was more excited than I was, which took me by surprise. She thanked me for reaching out. She said there's a new hire orientation class starting January 26, 2015. I told her I had already booked my flight and will be arriving on January 9, 2015.

Do you see how God can arrange things to work out for your good if only you believe and are sensitive to His voice directing you? She scheduled me for an interview the next day upon my arrival. I had to use what I had in savings to transport us, our personal belongings, and my car from Texas to New Jersey. Anyway, my interview went well, which was more like signing new employee paperwork.

I arrived as scheduled with no money, and my sister was kind enough to host me and my three children at the time. My sister lived in a one-bedroom apartment with her two children. Although she would have loved to host us as long as it required, her living space was just not big enough. After about a week of staying at her place, I went in search of an apartment that would accommodate myself and my children. As God could have it, I found an apartment within walking distance from her place. I met with the leasing agent, and we went over the lease agreement and the security deposit requirement, with a move-in date of January 11.

I explained to her that I moved back from Texas from an abusive marriage. I have a high-risk pregnancy with three minor children. I told her my children and I are currently residing with my sister and her two children in a one-bedroom apartment and that I have secured a job with a start date of January 26.

If you believe and have faith in God, He can make the impossible possible for you. Proverbs 21:1 (KJV) says, "The king's heart is in the hand of the Lord, as the rivers of water; He turns it to any place He will." The LORD has the power to turn the heart of anyone to fulfill His will for your life.

Needless to say, the leasing agent said she would approve me if I got a letter from my employer stating I was hired, with the start date and pay rate, and come up with the security deposit. As God could have it, I got the letter from my hiring manager, but I had no clue how I would come up with the security deposit. My parents and siblings were not in the position to assist me with the amount of money I needed. I made a couple of phone calls, and God moved the heart of a friend to provide the amount needed as a gift.

I made the deposit as requested, signed a one-year lease agreement, and moved on February 15. God is more than able to move mountains for you unto His glory. He is your all-sufficient God. Because in this day and age, who would allow you to lease out a place and to move in based on a letter of employment? It had to be God. Just like He turned the heart of Cyrus, king of Persia, to make a proclamation in fulfillment of His Word spoken through Jeremiah in Ezra 1:1, He can do the same for you.

That scripture says,

> Now in the first year of Cyrus king of
> Persia, that the word of the LORD by the mouth
> of Jeremiah might be fulfilled, the LORD stirred
> up the spirit of Cyrus king of Persia, that he made

a proclamation throughout all his kingdom, and
put it also in writing, saying. (Ezra 1:1 KJV)

The Lord can stir up the heart of anyone He chooses to do anything for you to fulfill His promises over your life. Promises that you will not lack any good thing, that you are the head and not the tail, that you are more than a conqueror, that you are blessed going out and coming in. Promises of healing, protection, and deliverance to name a few. You only need to believe in Him and make a conscious decision to walk in His ways. Start by establishing a true personal relationship with God by allowing the Holy Spirit to transform your heart, and begin to take an obedient walk of faith.

So family and friends continued to be a blessing to me and my children financially to put food on our table. I started working on January 26 as scheduled. After settling in my new apartment and work, I met with a divorce attorney and had divorce papers prepared. I knew I did not want to go back to a toxic relationship. Because my pregnancy was high risk, I had to be seen by my obstetrician weekly along with weekly ultrasounds. I was experiencing a tremendous amount of stress, so I decided to pause the divorce process and focus on getting through my pregnancy and delivery.

Every week, the doctor visit or ultrasound showed one abnormal finding or another for which hospital admission for monitoring was required. I was so afraid that I would lose my baby. Imagine, I just started this new job, not even close to completing my ninety-day probationary period, and neither did I start accumulating vacation time.

My first month's rent was approaching. How was I going to pay this rent, let alone feed my children? On some days, I would not eat because there was only enough to feed my children.

If you are reading this book, know that God speaks. Even in your darkest moments, He speaks. He is always speaking to us, but we are not spiritually inclined to hear and know His voice. We are oftentimes looking for a loud, audible voice. Zechariah 4:6 tells us that God's work is "not by might nor by power, but by My Spirit."

He is God, and He chooses how He wants to speak to you. Usually, it's still and quiet. So the LORD directed me to go back and speak with the leasing agent. I prayed and asked the LORD to go ahead of me. I went as instructed. I informed the agent that I started working as planned, but my first pay will be in three weeks, and I will not be able to pay my first month's rent when it is due.

See what God can do when He is with you. I was in awe of what she told me. She asked me to let her know when I will be able to make the payment. I informed her of the date. As I was leaving, she said, "When the date is drawing near, and you need an extension, just let me know." What a miracle of God!

So after the frequent hospitalizations and bed rest, I made it to seven months in my pregnancy. I went for my weekly ultrasound, and it showed that the amniotic fluid around the baby was very low, a little over four liters, and the baby has a critically low fetal heart rate. I was informed that I was going to be admitted for observation, bed rest, and fluid replacement. I informed my father, and he came to the hospital right away. I was taken to the prenatal floor. I was immediately connected to the fetal heart monitor because of my baby's critically low heart rate.

I remembered being placed in different positions with no improvement. To avoid further complications or fetal demise, I was rushed in for an emergency cesarean section. So my baby was delivered at seven months, weighing only four pounds and seven ounces. She was immediately taken to the neonatal intensive care unit for monitoring and support. Her heart and lungs were still very fragile. She had prolonged pulses in her breathing, could not keep her body temperature to where it needed to be, and had some gastrointestinal issues. Her stomach would be so distended as if it would pop open when touched.

Every time I saw her, I just broke down in tears. I could not bear to see my baby suffering. I was released from the hospital four days after she was born, but she had to remain in the hospital until she was stronger, and her symptoms improved.

Driving away from the hospital, leaving my baby, and imagining her being all alone in her hospital room were the most difficult thing

I have ever experienced. I cried all the way home and every day until she was released. Whenever I visited, the nurses and doctors would always tell me how surprised they were at her progress. They said her brain function greatly surpassed other premature babies born at her age. Scripture tells us to give thanks in all things—whether good or bad. The devil's strategy is to keep you focused on only the bad aspects of your situation. As a result, you lose sight of the workings of God in it.

There is always something good in every bad situation. Rest assured that God has a plan for you, and ultimately, He will work everything out for your good. Romans 8:28 says (KJV), "And we know that God causes all things to work together for good to those who love God, to those who are called according to His purpose." As God could have it, my baby was released home from the neonatal intensive care unit after a two-week stay with no complication, unto His glory.

Chapter 7

Another Chance

My husband decided to come back. He came along with a pastor to speak on his behalf, who begged me to give him another chance. Having experienced all that I went through with the pregnancy and what my baby endured as a result of the stress and trauma I endured at his hands, I had a lot of reservations. But because of my fear of God and my moral values as a child of God, I decided to once again give him another chance. He again suggested that we move to Delaware since the move to Texas did not work out as planned. His reason was that Delaware was closer enough to both of our families.

The pastor who he brought to speak on his behalf had started a new church there and agreed to carry us through counseling. Because of those reasons and my wanting to do whatever it takes to make my marriage work, I agreed. We started driving to Delaware from New Jersey every Sunday for church services prior to the move. Looking back, I believe it was all part of his manipulative plan to regain control over my life because he also came as if he was literally having chest pains, holding his chest and stumbling over, to gain my sympathy. But God has a way of making what the enemy planned for evil to work out for good.

He convinced me not to inform anyone of our decision to move, not even my parents or sisters, and that we should change our phone numbers and not share them with anyone either. Little did I know that those rules were only applicable to me, as I later found out that he did the opposite by informing his family. He changed his phone number but redistributed it to all his contacts. Anyhow, we moved to Delaware in August of 2015. In September of that same year, I found out I was pregnant. We continued going to church as a family, faithfully every Sunday. As a matter of fact, he even became an usher in the church, something he had not done before. So in my heart, I was thankful to God for the change. Little did I know, I was soon going to get a "rude awakening" as the saying goes.

In December of that same year, while three months pregnant, God exposed a major incident that He had been doing secretly for years. The Lord is the alpha and omega (the beginning and the end). He knows the end from the beginning and works in times and seasons. God's plans are different from your plans, but His plans are always the best. To prevent what could potentially happen in the future, God allowed me to remain in the marriage until this incident was exposed. The fact that you may not understand God's workings does not mean that it will not work out for your good in the end. You only have to believe in Him.

Oftentimes, we pray to God to expose whatever it is in the dark concerning our lives and our situations and expose the plan of the enemy, to let it be exposed and so forth. But we forget to ask God for the grace to handle and accept what He exposes and the grace to get through or out of it. So here I was, devastated, confused, and hurt again; hate, unforgiveness, and resentment started building up in me. But I knew it wasn't of God, but I couldn't help myself. Why did I ever think that things would be different!

Here I was—down on the same path all over. So I did a twenty-one-day fast and prayer for help, mercy, and direction while pregnant. This went over until 2016. In addition to going to church, I was connected to a virtual ministry called Global Praying Family where we connect via a prayer line six days a week to stand by one another in prayer, study the Word of God, and discuss how we can apply it to our everyday lives, of which I'm still a member of. It has greatly transformed my life and strengthened my relationship with God.

During that time of fasting, I made a request to God. I asked God to show me a specific sign by our ten-year wedding anniversary if my husband is indeed the husband He has chosen for me. This sign was something only known between the LORD and me.

A year after that request, in September 2017, three days to my ten-year wedding anniversary, instead of the specific sign I asked God to show me, He exposed something very devastating yet again. I found out that my husband had an affair with one of the girls from the church we were attending as a family, and she had a set of year-old twins with him. Imagine the pain! I felt as though someone had taken a knife and stabbed me directly in my heart. Millions of different emotions were running through my body at the same time. My body was shaking as a leaf.

It was nighttime, not thinking rationally, I jumped in my car with the intention of driving to his mistress's house to ask her why. Why would she choose to hurt me the way she did? But the whole point was silly because I did not even know where she lived. So I decided to call the pastor from the virtual ministry who encouraged me in the Lord and advised that I go back home, which I did. I had endured so much pain already throughout the marriage that I was still recovering from, so this hit me really hard.

I cried for days and nights with no appetite to eat, drink, or sleep. I had no family or friends in Delaware for support. Not knowing how my parents or siblings will react and trying to avoid the embarrassment of the situation, I did not tell anyone about it. I remember just wrapping my arms around my own body, in my closet, in an attempt to fulfill an embrace from a loved one. I just wanted to hear those words that, "It will be okay. You will get through this."

Our Father in Heaven assures us that He will never leave us nor forsake us. He tells us in Isaiah 43:2 (KJV),

> When thou passest through the waters, I will
> be with thee; and through the rivers, they shall
> not overflow thee: when thou walkest through
> the fire, thou shalt not be burned; neither shall
> the flame kindle upon thee.

He always positions a helper for us in our time of need. We only have to look beyond the circumstance or situation. For me, in this time, my helper was my Bible and Pastor Akhmed who He chose to use to carry me through this, to encourage me, and to give me hope. May the Lord remember him for obeying His call.

At this point, I was like, "God, what is going on? What have I done to deserve all of this? What is happening to me? Why me?" I stopped going to church, but by the grace of God, I continued my relationship with Him outside the church through the praying ministry and spending personal time with Him. But I was not fulfilled. I felt something was missing, and I needed to get back in church.

Chapter 8

God, I Need to Hear from You!

On the advice of Pastor Akhmed from the praying ministry, I decided to take time off work to seek God for answers yet another time. We always have to seek God for direction in everything we do to know what His will is. When you find yourself at crossroads in life and not sure how to proceed, seek the Lord through prayer, and you will hear His voice.

Isaiah 30:21 (KJV) says, "And thine ears shall hear a word behind thee, saying, This is the way, walk ye in it, when ye turn to the right hand, and when ye turn to the left." So the first week in December 2017, I took a week off work, without pay, to seek the face of God in fasting and prayer. I cried to God for mercy and asked Him some questions like "What part did I contribute to all of this? Help me, Lord, to remember that I may seek Your mercy." I prayed for direction that I may not make any hasty decision on my own. I prayed for the will of God for my life.

I said, "Father, even if I am crying every day asking You for something, if it is not Your will, please do not let my tears cause you to grant it to me. I want Your perfect, divine will for my life." I asked God to plant me in a church of His choosing, where His presence is and where He is being worshiped. I said, "God, I need to hear from You before these seven days are over. Show me something, or give me a Word."

Well, needless to say, we cannot demand God to do things for us when we ask for His will to be done. I completed the seven days, with no sign or word, or at least not what I was anticipating. However, I continued to trust in the LORD. The fact that we don't hear from God immediately every time we call upon Him does not mean that He is not listening or working on our behalf. Isaiah 59:1 (KJV) says, "Behold, the LORD's hand is not shortened, that it cannot save; neither his ear heavy, that it cannot hear."

Still depressed and in pain, the second week in December 2017, I met someone at my place of employment named Teju. I want to encourage someone to not let the circumstances you are going through cause you to take for granted any encounter you have with someone, no matter who they are or who you may know them to be because you never know if that person is an answer God has sent to that prayer or thing you've been believing Him for. Despite my situations, before I leave my house every morning, I ask God to use me to make a difference in someone's life, one way or another, however He chooses.

I met Teju by *divine arrangements* as she puts it, which I believe. We introduced ourselves. She asked based on my name, "Where are you from?"

I said, "Liberia. Where are you from [based on her name]?"

She said, "Nigeria."

I said, "Oh, that makes us sisters then."

We both agreed, and that first encounter that should have been no longer than thirty minutes lasted for over two hours. We talked, we laughed, and we cried together all to the glory of God.

I asked her, "What church do you attend?"

She said, "RCCG Amazing Grace. You should come one day and visit."

I asked, "How is the church? How is the pastor? Is it one of those churches that all you hear is prosperity preaching, or I prophesy you shall receive this or that, or sow this or that seed because I want to be in a place where my soul can be fed with the true Word of God."

She said, "No, you come and see. You will be blessed. I promise you it is not like that."

So I told her, "Well, I've been away from church for too long, and I need to get back, so text me the address, and my children and I will come on Sunday."

I visited the second Sunday in December, and it was an amazing experience. The praise and worship and the humility of Pastor and the children's ministry are what captured me. My children and I continued to visit every Sunday for the remainder of the month, until 2018, on and off.

I did not attend the New Year's Eve service for 2018. I remember waking up on New Year's day with this heavy feeling of guilt, so I gathered my children together for prayer. After we prayed and thank God for the old year and for crossing us over into the new year, they all disbursed, and I was alone in the living room. I turned the TV on, went to YouTube, and started searching for RCCG Amazing Grace New Year's Eve service.

While searching, something drew my attention to previous year's New Year's Eve service from the branch in Dubai. I watched the entire program. At the end, the pastor instructed the congregation to take the last five minutes, to just worship and appreciate God.

He said, "Don't ask for anything. Just worship the Almighty God."

I was sitting on my couch worshiping. I felt the presence of God so strong that I went down on my knees in worship, crying and continuing even after the five minutes. Believe me, true worship invokes the presence of God and causes shaking in any situation. This is evidenced by the story of Paul and Silas in prison. Scripture tells us that at midnight, they began to pray and sing hymns to God, and their worship caused a sudden earthquake that shook the prison; their shackles fell off, the walls came down, and they were free to go (Acts 16).

Every one of us will face hardships, challenges, and difficulties in life. But when it happens, how you respond determines the outcome. These situations come to test our faith and loyalty in God, and when we were worshiping Him in church, we must truly mean it. It is easy to worship God when things are going well, but will you be able to do the same in those difficult times? It's because there are people who will be watching you and develop an opinion about God on the basis of your life and how you will respond.

Anyway, by the end of that week, on January 8, 2018, about four weeks after my time of prayer and supplication, I experienced another amazing encounter from the LORD. I dialed into the prayer line for the 8:00 p.m. session and put my phone on mute, which I usually do because of the noise in my background from my children. I heard the pastor ask two different people to give an opening prayer but got no response.

After a few minutes, he said, "Sister Jiangy, please lead us in a short prayer so we can begin."

I prayed quickly, put my phone back on mute, and went about preparing dinner. Unbeknownst to me, the pastor welcomed a guest pastor to take over. People of God, believe me when I tell you, the Almighty God is real. He knows our beginning and our end. There is nothing hidden about us that our God does not know even the secret things about our lives God knows. He cares about us and loves us very much. I stand here as a living testimony.

Remember, this is a virtual ministry. I've never met or spoken to this pastor before. I'm a very private person. But hearing God speak through him and say, "Tell my daughter her divine appointment has come, and I chose her while she was in her mother's womb," and so forth was the greatest feeling ever. The entire one-hour session was God speaking to me through His servant.

I don't know about you, but hearing the Almighty God, Creator of all, refer to me personally as His daughter is enough reason for me to dedicate my entire life to Him. He said I should remain in His Words and remain in His presence. So after over a month of waiting for a word or sign from the LORD, HE spoke through His servant.

As I continued attending this church of God, I prayed and asked God to show me a sign if His presence is not in Amazing Grace Church or if He is not being worshiped there because I don't want to be contaminated by any contrary spirit. I want to be planted where He and only Him alone is being worshiped. From 2017 until now, if my recollection is right, God has not shown anything to indicate that His presence is not in RCCG Amazing Grace.

I remembered one Sunday in 2018 I was getting my children ready for church. My husband had never visited the church. I never gave him the address because he never asked. Out of nowhere, he said he was going to some church near where we live.

I said to myself, *This may not end well,* thinking he may try to stop me from bringing the children. So while he was in the bathroom, the children and I hurriedly left the house. While driving, I silently prayed in my heart because I didn't want my children to hear me. I said, *Father, You said I should remain in Your Word and remain in Your presence. You also said I should introduce You to the children You have given me. I asked You to plant me in a church of Your choosing. Father, if it is the church I am coming from, redirect my steps back. If it is Amazing Grace where I am going, may Your Holy Spirit order my husband's step to Amazing Grace. If neither of these two churches is where You want us to be planted, then I ask that You direct us, in Jesus's name.* People of God, believe it or not, while sitting in the service, I looked back and saw my husband walking into the service. God is real, and He answers prayers.

Chapter 9

My Deliverance

There were so many unresolved issues in my marriage. I could not catch a break. Every time I was starting to heal from one situation, another occurred. I was constantly grieving. I felt like I was living, but my life had been sucked out of me. At this point, in 2018, eleven and a half years of marriage, twelve-plus years of relationship, it dawned on me that this marriage is not God's purpose for me. "The blessings of the LORD makes rich, and he adds no sorrow with it" (Proverbs 10:22 KJV).

He had given me enough signs, and I knew I had to find a way to get out. But how? Where do I start? How am I going to manage as a single mother with now five children? To make matters worse, I found out I was pregnant for my sixth child in December of 2018. When I informed my husband, he said when the baby is born, he will decide if he is the father or not. He made the same comment with all the other children. I felt like a failure. I felt betrayed in all sense of the word. The entire prime of my life had been wasted, including my time and resources. I cried myself to sleep almost every night and during the day as well. To make matters worse, my pregnancy was at high risk due to my age, and it was compromised by gestational diabetes.

Still in my first trimester, I was so sick with early pregnancy symptoms and my body adjusting to the diabetes medication I was taking. Seeing my condition, he decided it was the best time to make a trip to Africa for a month, which he did without a mutual agreement. He booked his ticket and departed on February 1, 2019. Again, my sorrow continued. Here I was, with a high-risk pregnancy, dealing with first-trimester pregnancy symptoms, my body adjusting to new medications, working full time, and taking care of four minor children. My only consolation and source of hope was the Lord and being in His church. It felt like during that time, every message preached was God comforting me, reassuring me, or pointing out where I went wrong. Sitting in the congregation, I remembered fighting back tears, sometimes not being able to control my tears.

On March 13, 2019, around 1:30 a.m., I heard my phone ringing. On the caller ID, I saw the name of one of the affiliate pastors of Global Praying Family Ministry, who I will refer to as Pastor Jacob. This was not someone I spoke to regularly. As a matter of fact, I had only spoken to him on two or so other occasions prior and not related to any personal issue. So when I saw the call, I was wondering, *Why was he calling me this early?*

I was deeply asleep, so by the time I could reach to answer the call, it stopped ringing. I decided to return the call when I was fully awake in the morning. Needless to say, I returned the call, but there was no answer. I proceeded to do my normal morning routine. I remembered being in the kitchen, washing dishes, and just grieving inside from all the hurt, pain, and disappointment. As the tears were rolling down my cheeks, I heard the sound of my phone ringing, and it was the pastor returning the call. He apologized for calling me so early and proceeded to tell me the reason for his call.

He said he woke up at that time from a dream the Lord showed him concerning me. He said in the dream, the Lord told him his sister (referring to me) is grieving and what was he doing about it. He said in the dream, I was on the phone with him and explained everything I was enduring in my marriage. Without me telling him anything, he narrated exactly what I was experiencing, based on his encounter in the dream. This, to me, was the confirmation I had been waiting for from the Lord.

The Lord works in times and seasons. It is important to be spiritually sensitive to His timing to avoid unnecessary delays in your purpose or deliverance. When you proclaim that you trust in the LORD, it means trusting Him beyond all your doubts, limitations, weaknesses, fear of the unknown, and people's opinion of you and fully depending on Him. It means seeing what God sees concerning you. Scripture tells us in Romans 8:28 (KJV), "And we know that all things work together for good to them that love God, to them who are the called according to his purpose."

It is important to pray for the gift of discernment to discern the next move of God in your life and be alert to His divine timing. Many may consider what I am about to say controversial, but I beg to differ. When you see your life filled with one mishap or another, you find yourself constantly in a revolving circle of almost getting there but never getting there; or maybe your life is stagnant, start looking within your household.

I heard a sermon titled "Look Again" from a very close family friend Pastor Deyla. You are looking every day, but are you actually seeing? Are you seeing the details that God is showing in the situation you are facing?

I am not saying you should go about accusing anyone randomly, but rather, go to God in prayer. He is the revealer of deep and hidden things. It is in His Word in Jeremiah 33:3, "Call unto me, and I will answer you and show you things that you knew not of." Ask God to reveal and unmask who or what is the source of the troubles you are having in your life. Ask Him for direction on how to proceed and, most importantly, wait patiently to hear from Him.

For me, this was God's divine timing for my life to bring me out of the marital bondage I was entrapped in for almost twelve years. Even with this confirmation and discernment, I still had some underlying doubts and fears. Because here I was, four months pregnant, at high risk with gestational diabetes, injecting myself with insulin four times a day, and on oral diabetes medication. I had four other minor daughters to care for and a nineteen-year-old son, and I was working full time.

One can only imagine my fears and thought processes: *LORD, are You sure this is the right time? Who divorces while pregnant? What will people say about me? What will be their perception of me? Am I capable of caring for and raising six children as a single parent? How am I going to manage financially? How will I juggle the children's drop-offs and pickups from school and work full time? Everyone is going to be staring at and judging me at church.*

My delivery is a scheduled cesarean section. Who will be with be in the hospital? Who will help me during my recovery? I remember going to church and feeling so embarrassed and emotionally torn. All I would do was bury my face in my hands in tears the entire service. These were some of the many fears and questions that were running through my mind. But these are all the tricks of the devil. He comes to steal, kill, and destroy, so he plays on your mind to prevent you from seeing God working in your life in the midst of the storm, trials, and tribulations. This is his way of keeping you from fulfilling your divine purpose. It is in these times that you have to pull strength from the LORD.

He said we should lean not on our own understanding but to trust in Him. When you are weak, He is your strength. This is an assurance in the LORD. Remember, the saying goes, "When one door closes, another door opens." Where death ends, resurrection begins. You can only fulfill your purpose when you are where God wanted or intended you to be. If you are in the wrong marriage, wrong profession or career, wrong location, or even wrong frame of mind, your true and divine purpose can never be truly actualized.

In obedience to the leading of the LORD, I filed for divorce. As a child of God, it is often difficult to take this decision. Most at times, we are focused on the scripture in Mark 10:9 (KJV) that says, "What therefore God hath joined together, let not man put asunder." As a result, a lot of people remain trapped in abusive marriages.

I understand that every marriage comes with its own challenges and attacks from the enemy and may not necessarily be wrong. So what is important is to seek the LORD in prayer to know if your union was truly joined by Him.

Two months after filing, I was granted the divorce because he chose not to respond. This, again, proved to me that the children and I meant very little to him. Here I was, six months pregnant, five children, four of them eleven years old and younger, and divorced. I had less than five hundred dollars in both checking and saving accounts combined and with a poor credit score as a result of financial mismanagement in the marriage. The combined lease was expiring in two months, and I knew I had to move because I could not afford the rent.

Chapter 10

God Works in Miraculous Ways

Where do I start, Lord? What will I do? The children were already settled in the community. They have been in the school for four years, which was a block from the house. They had their friends in the neighborhood, and most importantly, they were stable. We had really great supportive neighbors. With everything they had witnessed and endured through the marriage and dealing with the divorce, I wanted to maintain some stability in their lives.

I searched outside the development, hoping to find a place more affordable. But no matter where I looked, I did not get a sense of peace. I was at a crossroad and so confused. Proverbs 3:6 (KJV) says, "In all thy ways acknowledge Him, and He shall direct thy paths." It is important to always trust in the Lord when you need to understand which direction you need to take, and He will direct your steps. Remember, this can only happen if your ways are pleasing to Him.

I sought the Lord in prayer, and He directed me to my current leasing office. I went into the office and explained my situation. I met with Paula, who advised me to submit a transfer application for a unit that would be available at the time my current lease expires. She drove me by the house, but we could not enter because it was still occupied. We went back to the leasing office, and I submitted the application. Upon leaving the office, the Lord led me to drive back to the place and speak His Word over it. I did as He instructed, and by His grace, I was approved for a place within my budget.

My move-out date was August 30, three weeks before my scheduled cesarean section. Through His strength, I managed to pack up for my children and me. Now that I was all packed, who will help me load and unload the boxes from the truck? Who will help me settle in and get the girls ready for school that would be starting the following week? I remember being so stressed and worried. Though I was praying and trusting the LORD to make a way, there were still doubts. I had no friends or family in the area, and my children were very young, and I had no money to pay for moving services.

Our Father, the Almighty God, is faithful even when your faith is shaken. Philippians 4:6–7 (NLT) says,

> Don't worry about anything; instead, pray about everything. Tell God what you need, and thank him for all he has done. Then you will experience God's peace, which exceeds anything we can understand. His peace will guard your hearts and minds as you live in Christ Jesus.

All you have to do is lay down your burden and hurt and come as you are. When your ways are pleasing to the LORD, there is nothing that He cannot do for you. He has the power to cause the hearts of men to favor you and move on your behalf. I rented a U-Haul truck and picked it up the morning of the move. The truck was parked in the driveway, and I was sitting and wondering how this move was going to happen. Just at that moment, my phone rang. I quickly picked it up. To my surprise, it was Pastor of RCCG Amazing Grace, asking me to text her both addresses because she was sending some of the youth boys from the church to help. She also said that two of the women from the church who lives in my neighborhood will be coming as well.

Within thirty minutes, they were all at my house. As if that wasn't enough, the LORD had another surprise for me. I received a text from my manager requesting both addresses. She said she was closing the office at noon and sending everyone over to help. Before we could end the conversation, some of my coworkers were already at my door, and one car after another came pulling up. And guess what? They came with dinner for my children and me to last us for two to three days so I did not have to worry about cooking.

The two sisters from the church were in awe of the favor of God upon my life. One of the sisters said to me, "Sis, whatever it is you are doing for the LORD, keep doing it. We often hear about the favor of God, but I have not experienced it in action until now."

Together, with my coworkers, they moved all my things to my new place and unboxed and organized everything to its rightful place. Every time I tried to assist, I was asked not to lift a finger but to just give them directions on where to put each item. I am not sure if you are understanding exactly what I am saying. Before they left, everything was organized—my kitchen, my children's closet, my closet, and all the bathrooms.

When I thought nothing could be better than this, the LORD had another surprise. The next day, I received a call from one of my coworkers that dinner will be delivered. It didn't stop there. I would hear a knock on my door, and when I would answer, Sister Funmi would be unloading her car with groceries for my children and me. If it was not Sister Funmi, then it was Sister Teju with groceries and my coworker Shadi sending restaurant-prepared dinner. How good it is to serve the LORD! He is faithful and will never disappoint you if you put your trust and hope in Him. To the glory of God, the move was completed successfully.

As I said earlier, my cesarean section was scheduled three weeks after my move. With no money to buy any essential supplies for the new baby, I resorted to calling on the LORD yet another time. God wants you to depend on Him. Again, through my job, He moved the heart of my now program manager toward me. She donated boxes of clothes from newborn up to two years, including a crib, a bouncer, and a walker. God is the supplier of all your needs.

So my mother and my younger sister, both living in different states from Delaware, requested time off from their various jobs to come on the day of my scheduled cesarean section. Well, I was still working full time. I was scheduled for a routine ultrasound two days prior to my surgery. I woke up like every other morning feeling *"outside my body."* I could do my routine activities the day before like making breakfast for my children and getting ready for school. It was very exhausting. I felt nauseous and extremely tired, had some contractions here and there, and could barely walk. I drove my then nine-year-old to the bus stop and could not make it out of the car to stand with her, which is something I did every morning. After she left, I dropped my four- and three-year-olds to their babysitter and drove to work. I got to work and informed my coworkers and manager about how I was feeling. I told them based on how I felt, I believe the baby might be arriving earlier than planned.

I said, "My mother and sister are coming on the day planned for surgery, so if the baby decides to come earlier, I will be alone in the hospital." I also let them know that I was having an ultrasound after work that day. My manager said that I should let her know what is decided at the ultrasound. I went for the ultrasound as scheduled, and as expected, the amniotic fluid around my baby was abnormally low. Since it was two days earlier to my scheduled cesarean section, I was sent to triage to be admitted for delivery of my baby.

I started to panic because my other children were still in school. Who would pick them up, make dinner for them, help with homework, get them ready for bed, and so forth? My daughters were only eleven, nine, four, and three years old at the time. Yes, my nineteen-year-old son was there, but there is only so much he can do as a boy for his sisters. I reached out to my sister Beletiah, who had already planned on coming two days later.

As God could have it, she informed her manager and was given permission to work from home. Just an hour away from me, she came quickly and stayed at my house. One problem solved, now I needed to focus on getting admitted to have my baby delivered. I sent a group text message out to my coworkers informing them that I was being sent to triage to be admitted. As I was checking in at the triage desk to register, I heard the elevator doors open. I looked behind me and saw, to my surprise, one of my coworkers (Taylor) getting off. She said they received instructions that I must not be left alone at any time until my baby was safely delivered. They created shifts to be with me, and they each selected a shift. They were instructed not to leave until their replacement arrived.

Can you see the workings of God? Trust that He can do the same for you. She stayed with me until my admission was completed, and I was waiting for the hospital escort to take me to the preoperative unit. Just in that time, her relief came, Julia, and Taylor left. Julia brought a Bible with her for me. She said she knew I had a relationship with God, and having my Bible was important to me so she decided to bring hers for me in case I did not have mine because I did not get the chance to go home prior to being admitted.

A true soldier never leaves home without a weapon. As a child of God, you are His warrior and should always travel with your weapon, which is the Holy Bible. "For the weapons of our warfare are not carnal" (2 Corinthians 10:4 KJV). I did have my Bible with me.

It is very important as a child of God for people to identify Christ in you and identify you with Christ. It must not come from your lips but rather from your lifestyle. Proverbs 27:2 (NKJV) says, "Let another man praise you, and not your own mouth; A stranger, and not your own lips."

Julia stayed with me, encouraging me until I was taken to the preoperative unit. My cesarean section was scheduled for ten o'clock that night, but it kept being pushed back due to complications with the case before me. It was now eleven o'clock, and Julia had to leave because she lived far and had to be at work the next day. Prior to her leaving, she was relieved by another coworker, Shadi. So by eleven-thirty that night, I was being wheeled to the operating room with Shadi by my side.

I updated my father, mother, and sisters and gave them Shadi's number. I informed them that Shadi will update them moving forward. By one minute past midnight, my baby was successfully delivered. Shadi stayed with me until I was taken to recovery. She stayed a little longer but had to leave because it was now two in the morning, and she too had to go to work later that morning. A few minutes after she left, I developed postpartum hemorrhage. This is when a woman has heavy bleeding after giving birth. It is a serious but rare condition that can cause a drop in blood pressure and signs of shock. If the bleeding cannot be controlled, it may require blood transfusion and/or hysterectomy.

Thank God for His divine intervention; it was controlled. I do not know the best way to say this, but when God says, "Do not worry," trust that He is in control. The LORD is faithful and able to grant you solace when uncertainty arises in your life. Sometimes, life can turn some uncertain and unexpected corners. Oftentimes, it can be very difficult to maintain a positive attitude about the future and faith in the LORD.

Whenever you are experiencing doubt concerning issues you are facing, whether it is disappointment, failure, challenges in marriage or divorce, issues with your children or childlessness, health problem, or other obstacles, consider turning to the LORD. This can be done through prayer and reading His Word. Scripture tells us in Hebrews 4:12 (NKJV),

> The word of God is living and powerful, and sharper than any two-edged sword, piercing even to the division of soul and spirit, and of joints and marrow, and is a discerner of the thoughts and intents of the heart.

In His Word, you will find hope, encouragement, strength, peace, rest for your soul, and guidance to bring you solace during scary times.

We were discharged after four days. A couple of days after being discharged, the church organized and performed my baby's naming ceremony and dedication service. I was on maternity leave for three months. During that time, my sisters and mother took turns staying with me until I was fully recovered. Then returning to work was getting closer, and again, I started to worry.

Here, I was in need of childcare for my three- and four-year-old daughters as well as my almost-four months old baby. There was no way I could afford the cost even with my full-time salary in addition to our other costs of living. I tried to devise a plan, but nothing was adding up. I kept trying to figure it out on my own. This was one of my weaknesses, always trying to plan ahead.

My son often teases me that all I do is think. He says I think too much into things, creating more stress for myself, which is true. By the end of the day, no one can solve any problem by themselves. As a believer, it is important to look to the LORD for guidance. I was not totally trusting in the God of impossibility who has proven, time and time again, that He is with and will never leave me. Proverbs 3:5–6 (KJV) says, "Trust in the LORD with all thine heart; and lean not unto thine own understanding. In all thy ways acknowledge Him, and He shall direct thy paths."

While I was busy worrying, God had already arranged a solution without any effort on my part. My wonderful, caring, loving, and supportive pastor, stopped by to pay us a visit. During that visit, she asked concerning what I was going to do in terms of childcare for my three younger children once I returned to work. I said I honestly have no clue. I have been trying to wrap my head around it, but it is not adding up.

She paused and said, "You know, I run a daycare at the church. I am looking at the distance for you in the morning since the church is a bit far from you. But if the distance will not be an issue, you can bring the children to the daycare." And by the grace of God, she took the children and worked out a payment plan that fitted my budget. What a blessing! But no amount of money can buy the love, care, attention, and prayers my children received at Mercy Land Academy under Pastor Adeola and her staff.

To this day, my children still refer to her as their pastor and get excited every time they see her. So my three younger daughters attended the daycare center from December 2019 to March 2020. In March 2020, COVID-19 was declared a global pandemic, and there was a nationwide shutdown on schools, businesses, and places of worship. Being a registered professional nurse, I am considered a first-line worker and could not stay but had to go to work. Things opened back up briefly in April for childcare centers for first-line workers. Months went by quickly, and the 2020–2021 academic school year was fast approaching.

Due to the rising death toll from the coronavirus, a federal mandate was issued to keep all schools doors closed. All in-person classes were canceled and moved to distance learning in the new school year because of the pandemic. For the school year, I had one daughter entering seventh grade, one daughter entering fifth grade, one daughter entering kindergarten, one daughter pre-K four, and my baby in daycare. I was so confused and worried.

As a registered nurse and in my practice setting, working remotely was not an option. I provide direct care to dialysis patients whose lives depend on their treatments to survive. I also need the income to provide for my children and me. So there was no way that I could maintain my job and be home for my children's virtual learning at the same time. I consulted my Father in Heaven for direction, the God who knows the end from the beginning.

Whenever you pray, it is very important to ask God for spiritual sensitivity so you don't miss His answer. God can choose to respond to you in any way—whether through dreams, a family, friend, child, or even a sign. Jesus said, "My sheep listen to my voice; I know them, and they follow me" (John 10:27). So I believe it was in July 2020 that I received a call from one of the ladies who worked at the day-care center at the church to check on the girls. The girls loved her so much! She encouraged me to look for a prekindergarten program for my four-year-old daughter in order to prepare her for kindergarten. I had some reservations because as much as I thought it was a great idea, I knew I would not be able to afford the cost. I put it into consideration. I contacted several childcare centers within my area to inquire about availability for the three younger girls but to no avail. They were either close, not accepting new applications, cost too high, or only had availability for one child. I did not want them separated.

I kept praying, looking, and calling. One day while driving, God drew my attention to this private Christian Academy. I glanced at the school but didn't give it much thought or attention because I knew it was out of my reach financially. I kept searching on the internet for childcare centers, and the academy popped up. I contacted the school to inquire about availability for the prekindergarten opening.

The lady at the end of the line said, "Yes, we do have an opening." She went on to give me a brief overview of the school. They are a Christian institution that ran from daycare to twelfth grade and so forth.

I said, "Wow, that is amazing!" I informed her that I have five daughters who fall in every level of the school: daycare, prekindergarten four, kindergarten, fifth grade, and seventh grade. She asked if I would like to be scheduled to come in for a tour, and I agreed.

When the day of the tour came, I remembered getting home from work and feeling really tired. It is important to not be ignorant of the devices of Satan. The Bible tells us that he is very crafty in his dealings and will use whatever or whoever he needs to use to derail you from the path of God. He can even use your very self. The devil kept playing on my mind, reminding me of *how tired I was, how I shouldn't waste my time on the school's staff because I could not afford the tuition, I should just call and cancel, and so forth.* I was about to give in to the voice of the devil. I picked up my phone and proceeded to call the school, then I heard the gentle voice of the LORD saying, "Just go for the tour. You never know what can come out of it."

So I ask, Whose voice are you listening to in your circumstances? Sometimes, God speaks to us in a still small voice.

Reluctantly, I went for the tour. I was received with respect, despite going in as a single mother, and given a tour of the entire campus—from daycare to high school. Words are inadequate to express how impressed I was! The hallways and walls were filled with inspirational and motivational scriptures for the children. I could feel a sense of peace in the atmosphere. At the end of the tour, she said that the dean of the school had not left for the day. For some reason, he stayed late, and she would take me over to meet with him.

Wow! Do you see how God arranges things? God has the power to compel people to change their decision or normal routine to accomplish His purpose for you.

I was taken to the dean's office and introduced to him. He asked what were my thoughts about the school? I told him that I was very impressed and that I have always wanted my children to attend a school where the Lord is the center of the education. I said my children are well-behaved, God-fearing, and honor roll students. I explained that I have nightly devotion with them. They each take turn leading, and we discuss how we can apply the principles of God in our daily lives. It has been my desire for my children to attend a Christian school where they are not discriminated against for their beliefs and stance with the LORD.

He then asked what would stop me from enrolling my children in the school. I said, "Honestly, the only thing that would prevent me is the financial aspect. I was recently divorced from a twelve-year toxic marriage. I am the sole caretaker and provider for my children. I am working part-time because of their care needs, trying to put the pieces of my life back together, and there is no way I could afford the cost."

Remember Romans 8:28 (KJV) that says,

> And we know that God causes all things to
> work together for good to those who love God,
> to those who are called according to His purpose.

Well, indeed, He is faithful to His word.

The dean immediately grabbed a notepad and a pen. He asked me to give him my full name, contact information, and the names of all the children. He said, "Yes, we are an institution, with staff that needs to get paid, but we are first a ministry, and I will do everything in my power to ensure that your family is a part of this school."

I started saying, "*Thank You, LORD. To God be the glory!*"

I thanked him and the lady for the tour and left.

The next day, I received a call from the director of marketing, admissions, and special events to schedule an admission interview.

God does not look at your limitations. God's promises are unlimited. When you project your human limitations on God, it simply means you have a limited concept of who God is and His capabilities. Jesus said, "All things are possible to him who believes"

(Mark 9:23). Instead of trusting in the unlimited power of God, I was looking at my own limitations.

I told the lady that I do not think that would be necessary because I know I cannot afford it, and I did not want to waste her time or mine.

She said, "How about you come in, and after the interview, you can meet with the business manager to discuss the financial aspect. There may be some help available."

After consideration, I agreed to schedule the admission interview. I was instructed to bring all the girls for the appointment. The appointment date arrived, and my girls and I went as scheduled. They were all interviewed except for my daughter in daycare. After the interview, I was taken to meet with the business manager. We discussed my income and some numbers, which was not possible for me. She suggested that I complete the financial assistance application online, and we will discuss it further once it is completed.

After the interview and meeting with the business manager, my girls and I proceeded to leave. We got in our vehicle, and as I started to drive off, the LORD reminded me of the scripture that says,

> Every place that the sole of your foot shall
> tread upon, that have I given unto you, as I said
> unto Moses. (Joshua 1:3 KJV)

The LORD silently instructed me and ordered my steps to drive around the grounds of the school, declaring this scripture and personalizing it with each of the girls' names. I obeyed, drove around the campus three times, calling each of my daughter's names, and declaring as He, God, has allowed each of their feet to tread upon the grounds of the school and enter the school building so may they possess it according to His Word, in Jesus's name.

I thanked the LORD for bringing it to pass, and we left to return home. The next day, I received the link for the financial aid application, but I kept hesitating. I was finally able to get the application completed and submitted it. After submitting, I received a call from the business manager that evening. We discussed different amounts that were still way above what I could afford. I remained honest and open about my financial situation. Unfortunately, we could not agree on an amount that was affordable for me, and time was far spent. She suggested that we rest and sleep over it and allow God to help us come up with a decision that will work for my family.

To my surprise, she asked if she could pray with me. Knowing that prayer is how we communicate with God, and He said in Matthew 7:7, "Ask and it shall be given unto you," I gladly accepted. I don't remember her exact words, but she asked God for strength for me as a single mother and the grace to make the right decision. The next morning, I received a call from the business manager and was given an offer that was favorable for my family.

Some may call this mere coincidence, but I call it the divine favor of God. I also learned a few lessons from this entire process. The first lesson is that obedience is better than sacrifice. As it is written, "Hath the Lord as great delight in burnt offerings and sacrifices, as in obeying the voice of the Lord? Behold, to obey is better than sacrifice, and to hearken than the fat of rams" (1 Samuel 15:22 KJV). The second lesson is that there is power in declaring the Word of God by faith according to Romans 10:17 (ESV), "So faith comes from hearing, and hearing through the word of Christ." Also, Proverbs 18:21 (ESV) says, "Death and life are in the power of the tongue, and those who love it will eat its fruits." Lastly, no matter the circumstances you are facing, how difficult, impossible, or challenging it may be or seem, keep on trusting in the LORD, believe in His Word, and pray. At the end of it all, He will make everything work together for your good (Romans 8:28).

Right now, as I am writing this book, I can testify that I am living by the grace of God. How I am managing as the sole caretaker and provider for six children, five of which are thirteen years old and under, in the United States with a part-time income and no other assistance is only by the grace of God. I give Him all the glory.

Every day, He allows me and my children to experience what it means to be fully dependent on the LORD. There is a marked deficit in my monthly income to expenditures. I mean household needs. But someway, somehow, God makes it work that all of our bills are paid every month. Even the vehicle He provided for us has over eight thousand dollars in needed repairs. The engine light comes on every now and then. Every time it does, I lay hands on the car and remind Him of His promise to take care of us, and He keeps His promises every time. The car runs smoothly as if it was not a fourteen-year-old car.

If you make a conscious decision, without anyone coercing or persuading you to confess and repent of your sins, accept Jesus Christ of Nazareth as your LORD and personal Savior, and ask for the Holy Spirit to guide you to walk in the ways of the LORD, He will remain faithful to you. He will keep His promise to never leave you nor forsake you (Hebrews 13:5). He will keep His promise in Isaiah 43:2 (NKJV) that "when you pass through the waters, I will be with you; And through the rivers, they shall not overflow you. When you walk through the fire, you shall not be burned, Nor shall the flame scorch you." The LORD will remain faithful to all His promises for your life according to His will.

As you read throughout this book, my journey in life has been filled with many tribulations from my birth until now. How I came out of a twelve-year abusive marriage while pregnant, raising six children as a single parent, completed my master's degree in nursing, and working, it is only by the grace of God. He said that where we are weak, He is our strength.

Chapter 11

Conclusion and Encouragement

I end this book with Psalm 30:11–12 (NKJV),

> You have turned for me my mourning into dancing; You have put off my sackcloth and clothed me with gladness. To the end that my glory may sing praise to You and not be silent. O Lord my God, I will give thanks to You forever.

I am grateful to the LORD, for His mercy never fails me, and He continues to hold my children and me in His hands. I will continue to sing of His goodness in my life. From the time of my conception, He has been faithful and good to me. His voice led me through all the fires and storms of my life. He has been with me in the darkest moments of my life when there was no one or nowhere to turn. He is my excellent Father and my friend. I can testify that I live in the goodness of God.

Today, I am in this great land of the United States of America. God has put me in a position where I train doctors, nurses, lawyers, and people of various backgrounds, races, cultures, and statuses in my role as a registered nurse how to perform life-sustaining therapy in the comfort of their homes. People whose lives depend on the training, care, monitoring, and interventions I provide.

The Lord made me very fruitful and blessed me with six beautiful children—Kendrick, twenty-two years old; Gianna, now fourteen years old; Gabrielle, twelve years old; Kiersten, seven years old; Kristi, six years old; and Hannah, three years old. Sometimes I ask the Lord what is it about me that He entrusted me with such precious souls, and I ask Him to help me not to disappoint Him.

Sometimes, I grow weary in every capacity of the word and wonder when will my change come. I am always running in one direction or another. Then He reminds me that these are my sacrificial years. He renews my strength daily. He said that children are a blessing and not a curse.

> Behold, children are a heritage from the LORD, the fruit of the womb is a great reward. Like arrows in the hand of a warrior, so are the children of one's youth. Happy is the man who has his quiver full of them; they shall not be ashamed, but shall speak with their enemies in the gate. (Psalm 127:3–5 NKJV)

Remember, "Life is not about waiting for the storm to pass. It is about learning to dance in the rain" (unknown author). Your trials are the training ground for your victory.

> But by the grace of God I am what I am: and His grace which was bestowed upon me was not in vain; but I laboured more abundantly than they all: yet not I, but the grace of God which was with me. (1 Corinthians 15:10 KJV)

Everyone's waiting time is different. Yours may be one month, and another maybe a year. Yet another may be several years, like the children of Israel. You don't have to let the place of feeling, depressed, and defeated be the place you stay. As you go through life, God opens and closes doors all to His glory. I pray the LORD give you light and gladness and joy and honor as He did for the Jews in Esther 8:17 and as He is doing for me.

As He turned my tests into testimonies and my trials into triumphs, so He can do the same for you if only you believe. Do YOU BELIEVE?

God be glorified!

About the Author

Jiangy C. Moore, MSN, RN, CNN, was born and raised in Liberia, West Africa. Jiangy is a registered professional nurse and practices in Delaware. Jiangy is a mother of six beautiful children who she cherishes very much. She considers her faith, relationship with the Lord, and family to be most important to her. If she isn't practicing, you can almost always find her around her children. Jiangy is a survivor of a brutal civil war in Liberia, West Africa. She enjoys sharing her life testimonies and journeys with the Lord to encourage and strengthen others in faith.

If you were inspired by Jiangy's story, she would love to hear from you. You can share your testimonies with Jiangy at www.jiangycmoore.com.